CORNERSTONES OF FREEDOM™

NATIONAL INTELLIGENCE

BY ROBIN S. DOAK

CHILDREN'S PRESS®
An Imprint of Scholastic Inc.
New York Toronto London Auckland Sydney
Mexico City New Delhi Hong Kong
Danbury, Connecticut

BRINGING HISTORY to LIFE

Content Consultant
James Marten, PhD
Professor and Chair, History Department
Marquette University
Milwaukee, Wisconsin

Library of Congress Cataloging-in-Publication Data

Doak, Robin S. (Robin Santos), 1963–
   National intelligence/by Robin S. Doak.
      p. cm.—(Cornerstones of freedom)
   Includes bibliographical references and index.
   ISBN-13: 978-0-531-23061-9 (lib. bdg.)
   ISBN-13: 978-0-531-28161-1 (pbk.)
   1. Intelligence service—United States—Juvenile literature.
   2. Espionage, American—Juvenile literature. I. Title.
   JK468.I6D59 2012
   327.1273—dc23   2012000490

Printed in the United States of America 113
SCHOLASTIC, CHILDREN'S PRESS, CORNERSTONES OF FREEDOM™,
and associated logos are trademarks and/or registered trademarks of
Scholastic Inc.

1 2 3 4 5 6 7 8 9 10 R 22 21 20 19 18 17 16 15 14 13

Photographs © 2013: AP Images: 5 top, 26 (B.K. Bangash), 30 (Chao Soi
Cheong), 43 (Damian Dovarganes), 4 top, 10, 11, 28 (J. Scott Applewhite),
35 (Joe Marquette), 15, 58 (Julie Jacobson), 32 (Kyodo News), 36 (Manuel
Balce Ceneta), 2, 3, 34 (Mark J. Terrill), 54, 59 (Mary Altaffer), 5 bottom, 31
(Michael Conroy), 51 (Nasser Nasser), 44 (Pablo Martinez Monsivais), 39
(Rex Features), 21 (Richard Heyser private collection); 7, 22, 46, 50, 57 top;
Corbis Images/Bettmann: 38; Danita Delimont Stock Photography/Dennis
Brack: 27; Department of Defense/Cherie Cullen: 14; Getty Images: 6, 57
bottom (Chris Kleponis/AFP), 42 (David Bohrer), 48 (John Moore), 23 (Paul
J. Richards/AFP); Landov: 13 (Hamad I. Mohammed), 40 (Reuters); Library
of Congress/Augustus Weidenbach: 20; Media Bakery/StockTrek Images:
cover; Superstock, Inc./Everett Collection: 4 bottom, 18; The Image Works/
RIA Novosti: 24, 56; U.S. Navy/Petty Officer 2nd Class Joshua T. Rodriguez:
back cover; White House Photo: 55 (Chuck Kennedy), 8, 16, 17 (Pete Souza).

Maps by XNR Productions, Inc.

Did you know that studying history can be fun?

BRING HISTORY TO LIFE by becoming a history investigator. Examine the evidence (primary and secondary source materials); cross-examine the people and witnesses. Take a look at what was happening at the time—but be careful! What happened years ago might suddenly become incredibly interesting and change the way you think!

Contents

The Pursuit of Justice

President Barack Obama announces the death of Osama bin Laden in a televised address.

On May 1, 2011, a squad of U.S. Navy SEALs raided a secluded compound in Abbottabad, in northeastern Pakistan. The highly trained soldiers discovered **terrorist** leader Osama bin Laden hiding inside the compound.

During a quick gun battle, the world's most wanted terrorist was shot dead.

U.S. intelligence agents had tracked one of bin Laden's assistants to the Abbottabad compound in August 2010. In the following weeks, they worked to determine whether bin Laden himself was living in the compound.

After bin Laden's death, President Barack Obama praised the men and women of the U.S. national intelligence agencies. He said, "The American people do not see their work nor know their names. But tonight, they feel the satisfaction of their work and the result of their pursuit of justice."

Freedom from fear is a basic human right. It is the freedom to live each day without being afraid. It is the freedom to live in a secure environment. Intelligence agents play a key role in securing this freedom for all Americans.

Osama bin Laden's death brought a sense of closure to many Americans who were affected by the September 11, 2001, terrorist attacks.

AVY SEALS IN THE BIN LADEN RAID.

CHAPTER 1

WHAT IS NATIONAL INTELLIGENCE?

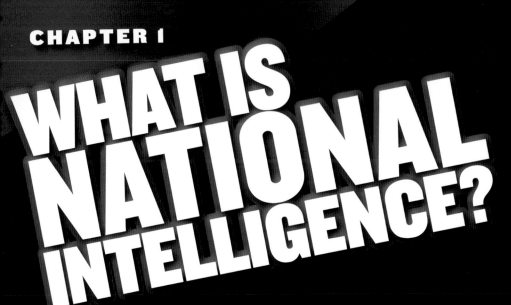

Intelligence agencies work closely with the president and other important government officials.

INTELLIGENCE IS INFORMATION that is gathered and analyzed by government agencies, and used to help the country's leaders make important decisions. Such information is often used to protect the United States, its citizens, and its interests. Good intelligence might help the government prevent terrorist attacks, win military battles, or catch spies.

Intelligence also helps government officials better understand the political, social, and economic situations in other countries. Is a foreign government trying to buy nuclear weapons? Is it harboring terrorists? The president and other leaders can use this information to create foreign policy.

John Brennan is President Obama's chief counterterrorism adviser.

Most of the activities that take place in intelligence agencies are top secret. Spies, secret agents, code breakers, and analysts work behind the scenes to obtain and understand information that others want to keep hidden. Other agents specialize in counterterrorism. This means they work to prevent foreign or enemy agents from stealing U.S. secrets. All intelligence agencies must always work within the laws of the United States.

The Intelligence Community

The United States has the largest and most expensive intelligence network in the world. Sixteen separate agencies are charged with finding and analyzing intelligence at home and abroad. Together, the agencies are known as the intelligence community (IC). Each year, the United States spends about $75 million and employs about 200,000 people to gather intelligence.

The IC is overseen by the Office of the Director of National Intelligence (ODNI). The ODNI was created in 2004 in response to the September 11, 2001, terrorist attacks. During investigations into the attacks, Americans learned that a number of intelligence agencies had pieces of information that might have prevented the disaster if the agencies had shared their findings with one another. Congress passed an act to try to prevent such a failure from ever happening again.

In 2010, President Obama selected James Clapper to be the new director of national intelligence.

THE INTELLIGENCE REFORM AND TERRORISM PREVENTION ACT OF 2004

The Intelligence Reform and Terrorism Prevention Act of 2004 created the ODNI and reformed U.S. intelligence. The act was passed after a lack of communication between intelligence agencies resulted in a failure to protect the country from the 9/11 terrorist attacks. See page 60 for a link to read the act online.

The director of national intelligence is the head of the ODNI. The director's job is to ensure that the agencies cooperate and share information with one another in a timely manner. The director also serves as the president's senior intelligence adviser.

To help make sure that all information is shared, the director oversees the Library of National Intelligence. The library contains information from all branches of the IC. The library's goal is to provide each agency with easy access to the information held by the others.

Intelligence Agencies

The 16 intelligence agencies are divided into three different groups: program managers, departmental components, and service components. The six program managers are among the best known of the intelligence agencies. In addition to collecting and analyzing intelligence, they also advise and assist the ODNI in many different ways.

The first program manager is the Central Intelligence Agency (CIA). The CIA is the largest producer of

The FBI works mainly within the borders of the United States.

information for the president and other policy makers. The Defense Intelligence Agency (DIA) is a program manager that collects and analyzes information related to military subjects. The Federal Bureau of Investigation (FBI) is an intelligence and law enforcement agency whose primary goals include stopping terrorism and cybercrimes. The National Geospatial-Intelligence Agency (NGA) is in charge of photographic intelligence. Its agents use equipment such as airplanes, **drones**, and satellites to collect information. The National Reconnaissance Office (NRO) designs, builds, launches, and maintains satellites.

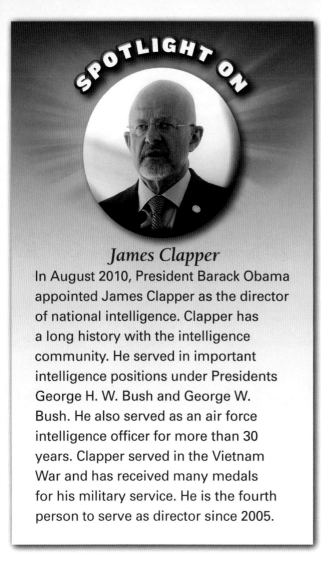

James Clapper

In August 2010, President Barack Obama appointed James Clapper as the director of national intelligence. Clapper has a long history with the intelligence community. He served in important intelligence positions under Presidents George H. W. Bush and George W. Bush. He also served as an air force intelligence officer for more than 30 years. Clapper served in the Vietnam War and has received many medals for his military service. He is the fourth person to serve as director since 2005.

Finally, the National Security Agency (NSA) is in charge of signals intelligence, or SIGINT. Signals intelligence is the interception of messages on radios, telephones, or other communication equipment. It also includes code breaking.

Five departmental components collect and analyze information for their own departments. They are the Departments of State, Energy, Homeland Security, Justice, and the Treasury. These departments have their own intelligence agencies. The Justice Department's intelligence agency works directly for its Drug Enforcement Administration. This group collects information that is used to stop illegal drug trafficking.

The service components intelligence agencies work for the five branches of the U.S. military. The army, navy, air force, marines, and coast guard each have their own agencies. Service agencies collect and analyze intelligence both at home and overseas.

The Drug Enforcement Administration works to prevent the sale of illegal drugs in the United States.

All of the agencies within the intelligence community share a common goal of obtaining information that will inform the president on global situations and allow him to make the best possible choices for the nation. Their top priority is to keep the United States safe and secure.

The Intelligence Cycle

The intelligence cycle is the process of collecting and analyzing the information that is important to U.S. security. The cycle is endless. Conditions throughout the world are constantly changing and evolving. In today's global society, even events in small, faraway nations can affect the United States.

There are five steps in the intelligence cycle. The first step is planning. Planning begins with the president and the National Security Council (NSC). The NSC includes the vice president, the secretary of state, the secretary of defense, and the assistant to the president for national security affairs. Together, the president and the NSC identify intelligence priorities. This is called threat assessment.

Not all of the issues identified as threats can be investigated. The world is a big place, and the intelligence community is limited by time, money, and manpower. The president and his advisers decide which threats should be investigated.

The second step in the intelligence cycle is collecting information. Once the targets have been chosen, the agencies begin to collect as much information as they can.

The third and fourth steps of the intelligence cycle

President Obama and the National Security Council watched a live video feed of the mission to eliminate Osama bin Laden.

The president carefully studies the reports prepared for him by intelligence agencies.

are processing and analyzing information. Experts within the agencies examine the information in its original form and convert it into intelligence that can be understood by all. Analysts then study the information and figure out what its importance might be. They create reports, briefings, and memos that help policy makers understand the intelligence.

The intelligence cycle's fifth and final step is the delivery of intelligence to the president. Every day, the president and other policy makers receive reports with the latest intelligence information. This allows them to do their jobs effectively.

CHAPTER 2

COLLECTING INTELLIGENCE

William "Wild Bill" Donovan was the director of the Office of Strategic Services during World War II.

THROUGHOUT HISTORY, government leaders have constantly searched for ways to learn more about their enemies. During the Revolutionary War, George Washington hired private spies to find out what the British army was planning. In the Civil War, Union soldiers sometimes rode in hot air balloons to watch Confederate activities.

The first centralized intelligence agency in U.S. history was founded during World War II. The Office of Strategic Services (OSS) pioneered the use of special spy equipment, including secret cameras and unusual weapons. It also took part in secret actions in other countries, including **sabotage** of enemy factories and airfields. The OSS was disbanded when the war ended.

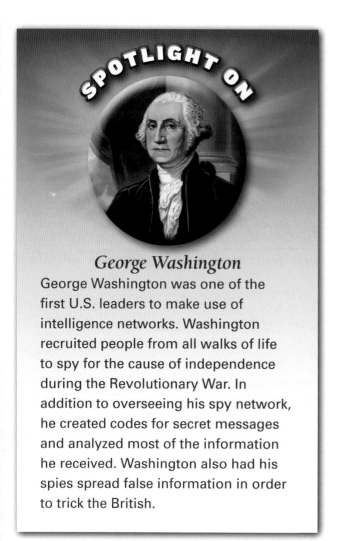

George Washington

George Washington was one of the first U.S. leaders to make use of intelligence networks. Washington recruited people from all walks of life to spy for the cause of independence during the Revolutionary War. In addition to overseeing his spy network, he created codes for secret messages and analyzed most of the information he received. Washington also had his spies spread false information in order to trick the British.

Modern Intelligence Collection

Intelligence took on even greater importance during the Cold War. The Cold War was a period of hostility between the United States and the Union of Soviet Socialist Republics (USSR) that lasted from around 1947 to 1991. During this time, the CIA was created to learn as much as possible about Soviet weapons, troops, and activities.

Each agency within the intelligence community has its own methods of collecting intelligence. Some specialize in using high-tech equipment to gather information. Others use secret agents and spies to **infiltrate** terrorist groups or foreign governments.

Modern intelligence is sometimes organized based on its source, or how the information is obtained. Sources can include human intelligence, signals intelligence, imagery intelligence, and open source intelligence.

Human Intelligence

Human intelligence (HUMINT) is any information that comes from human sources. This information could come from someone who is working in a foreign embassy. It could come from a tourist who observes something unusual while traveling in another country. It could even come from someone who sees suspicious activity in his or her own neighborhood.

HUMINT can also come from secret agents or spies. A spy is someone who is paid by one government to work undercover and get information about another

During the Cold War, President John F. Kennedy (right) used information gathered by air force spy planes to make important foreign policy decisions.

In 2008, it was revealed that about 24,000 people, including the famous chef Julia Child (above), had served as spies for the OSS.

government or group. Spies are often **foreign nationals**. For example, the United States might recruit a Chinese scientist to spy on his own country and deliver weapons or documents to U.S. agents.

Few people who work directly for U.S. intelligence agencies are spies themselves. Instead, they look for, recruit, and handle the spies in other countries. These people are sometimes called spy handlers or operations officers.

Why do people become spies? Some are motivated by money. Others are motivated by political or religious beliefs. For example, a foreign government official might agree to spy for the United States and infiltrate a terrorist cell because he strongly disagrees with his country's leader.

Human Intelligence Failures and Successes

Operations officers sometimes have difficulty finding good spies in other countries. The people who are most willing to spy are often not very trustworthy. They may be criminals or other people who lack a strong sense of right and wrong.

Animal Spies

Not all secret agents are human. During the 1960s, the CIA implanted a microphone and battery inside a cat in order to eavesdrop on people. The cat could not be trained to do what it was told, and the experiment was a failure. In the 1970s, the agency tested pigeons with tiny cameras strapped to their breasts. The details of this experiment are still **classified**. Like the microphone cat, the pigeon spies were unsuccessful.

As a result, human intelligence sometimes fails. In 2002, an Iraqi spy named Rafid Ahmed Alwan al-Janabi told German agents that Iraq had weapons of mass destruction. This information was passed on to the United States. U.S. leaders used this information to help justify starting a war with Iraq. It was later revealed that al-Janabi had lied.

Soviet intelligence officer Oleg Penkovsky's information was crucial to President Kennedy's negotiations with the Soviet Union.

Human intelligence can have spectacular results when it is successful. In 1961, a Soviet intelligence officer named Oleg Penkovsky began feeding documents and other information to British and American intelligence agencies. One crucial piece of intelligence from Penkovsky was that the Soviets were placing nuclear missiles in Cuba. President John F. Kennedy used this and other information to avoid a war with the Soviets. Like many spies, Penkovsky paid the ultimate price for his activities. In 1962, he was arrested by the Soviets and put on trial for **treason**. He was found guilty and executed in 1963.

Signals and Imagery Intelligence

Signals intelligence (SIGINT) is data that is intercepted from electrical communication systems such as telephones. It also includes data from radar and weapons systems. Experts use antennae, microphones, and other listening devices to collect communications intelligence. Special machines pick up data about enemy weapons by analyzing the signals emitted during a weapons test.

SIGINT became an important part of the war effort during World War II. In Operation Magic, U.S. intelligence agents intercepted Japanese communications. They were able to decode the messages and prevent several Japanese naval victories.

A FIRSTHAND LOOK AT
THE CIA'S PENKOVSKY MEMO

When CIA agents realized that Oleg Penkovsky was in danger of being killed by his own government, they attempted to convince the Soviet government to spare his life. See page 60 for a link to see an official CIA memo detailing the situation.

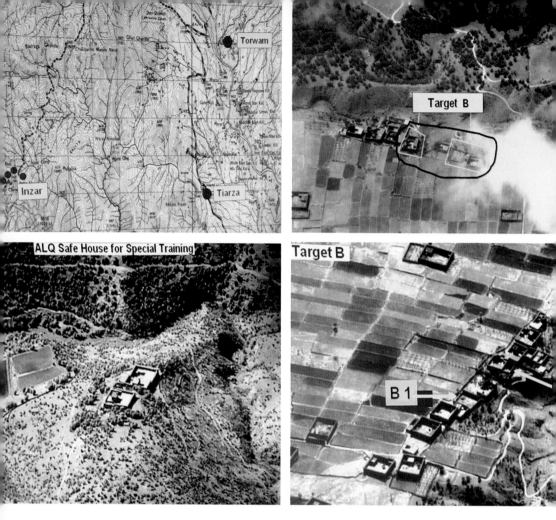

Satellite photos have helped military leaders identify many terrorist hideouts and training facilities.

Imagery intelligence (IMINT) is any intelligence that comes from visual sources such as photographs or maps. Intelligence agencies can use this information to better understand the physical features of foreign land. This type of intelligence is especially important in military operations.

Intelligence agencies collect IMINT using a variety of methods. Cameras mounted in space satellites can photograph suspected missile storehouses, army bases, or terrorist training camps. Satellite photos also allow intelligence agents to make highly accurate maps of remote areas. Spy planes and drones are also used to photograph targeted areas.

Open Source Intelligence

Not all intelligence is secret. Open source intelligence (OSINT) is information that is collected from the Internet, radio, television, newspapers, and other public sources. This type of information is readily available to anyone who looks for it. Agencies can gain important knowledge from public materials. The CIA runs the Open Source Center to search public sources for information that might prove valuable.

Intelligence agents collect a large amount of information from the Internet.

CHAPTER 3

INTELLIGENCE TODAY

The ODNI headquarters is located in McLean, Virginia, near Washington, D.C.

WHICH ISSUES ARE INTELLIGENCE
agencies working on today? Because of the secret
nature of information gathering, it is impossible
to pinpoint exactly where in the world agents are
collecting intelligence. But there are a number of
important issues that are likely among the IC's
top priorities.

The September 11, 2001, attacks made terrorism a major priority for the intelligence community.

Terrorism

After the attacks of September 11, 2001, many Americans realized for the first time that foreign terrorists could carry out deadly large-scale threats in America. In recent years, U.S. intelligence agencies have made terrorist groups such as al-Qaeda a top focus of their efforts.

Many branches of the IC play a role in the war on terrorism. The CIA, DIA, and FBI all work to stop terrorist activities in the United States and around the world. Agents at the ODNI's National Counterterrorism Center analyze information, set collection priorities, and find new ways to protect the nation from terrorist attacks.

Terrorism is difficult to combat. There are many groups throughout the world that want to harm the United States. These groups are constantly looking for ways to get past U.S. defenses. When one group is destroyed, another often rises to take its place. The IC will likely be fighting terrorism for many years to come.

SPOTLIGHT ON

The Terrorist Identities Datamart Environment

The Terrorist Identities Datamart Environment allows members of the IC to carefully track the activities of suspected terrorists. This huge database contains the names of those people suspected of being terrorists or helping terrorist groups. IC agents update the list every day. The database is then used to create the No-Fly List. People on the No-Fly List are not allowed to travel into or out of the United States on commercial airplanes. In March 2011, there were about 500,000 people on the list. Just 2 percent of these people were U.S. citizens.

Weapons of Mass Destruction

Another of the IC's goals is to stop the creation of weapons of mass destruction (WMDs). Such weapons include nuclear, chemical, and biological weapons that could cause large-scale devastation. The United States has been collecting and analyzing information about other nations'

WMD capabilities since the Cold War. Although the Cold War is over, intelligence about WMDs is more important than ever before.

Many nations have signed international treaties agreeing to stop WMD production. But others, including Israel and North Korea, refuse to sign these treaties. Experts worry that WMDs—or the materials or expertise used to build them—could fall into the hands of terrorist groups. These terrorists might then use the weapons to launch deadly attacks on their targets.

Some intelligence agencies keep an eye on the weapons programs of nations and terrorist groups. They work to track the number and strength of WMDs throughout the world. They also collect information on

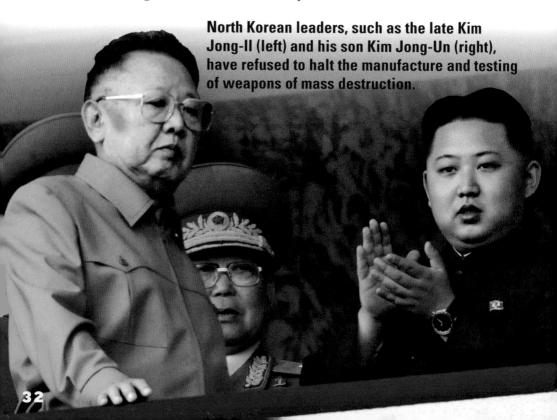

North Korean leaders, such as the late Kim Jong-Il (left) and his son Kim Jong-Un (right), have refused to halt the manufacture and testing of weapons of mass destruction.

nations and groups that may be selling or buying these dangerous weapons.

Cyberattacks

Cyberattacks are another major threat to the United States. Cyberattacks are attacks on computer systems, networks, and Internet sites. Because computers play such a key role in our daily lives, cyberattacks can have serious consequences.

Computers control electricity and other energy systems throughout the nation. Financial and medical information is stored in computer systems. Local, state, and federal governments use computers and the Internet for everything from storing employee information to controlling communication systems. As a result, a cyberattack could shut down the nation's entire **infrastructure**, from banks and businesses to hospitals and power grids.

Cyberattacks also put top secret government information at risk. In early 2011, **hackers** attacked

Senate and CIA Web sites. The attacks did not cause any damage, but they showed that these sensitive sites were not secure. In May 2011, U.S. government officials stated that they consider cyberattacks to be acts of war. This means that the United States could declare war on countries that attempt such attacks.

Counterintelligence

How does the IC keep its own secrets safe? **Counterintelligence** is the process of preventing foreign groups from stealing U.S. intelligence. For example, a terrorist group might try to discover where airport security is weakest in the United States. Or an enemy

Cybersecurity experts must stay up to date on the latest hacking techniques.

In 2009, former FBI deputy director Robert "Bear" Bryant was appointed national counterintelligence executive.

nation might launch a cyberattack to steal weapons information from a government computer system.

According to a recent government report, the United States is the top intelligence target for foreign intelligence agencies. In 2007, it was reported that 140 intelligence services from other countries were trying to gain access to U.S. secrets.

The Office of the National Counterintelligence Executive, part of the ODNI, coordinates all counterintelligence activities. It makes sure that all intelligence agencies work together to keep America's secrets safe.

CHAPTER 4

USING INTELLIGENCE

The IC relies on analysts to make sense of the information it gathers.

EVERY DAY, U.S. INTELLIGENCE agencies receive valuable information that could prove vital to protecting the nation. But such information is useless if government officials cannot understand its importance or what it means. Processing and analyzing are the steps in the intelligence cycle that convert raw data into usable intelligence.

Analysts sometimes accompany intelligence agents in the field so they can process new information as it is captured.

Making Information Meaningful

Processing information is the third step in the intelligence cycle. It involves translating collected information into an understandable form. If a document is in Russian, for example, language experts within the IC translate it into English. Other experts can help describe what is being shown in satellite images of enemy territory. Some intelligence agents specialize in decoding enemy messages.

Analyzing the processed information is the fourth step in the cycle. Expert analysts must decide what the information means, why it is important, and if it is reliable. They must also figure out whether the information could affect U.S. security or interests.

Finished intelligence is information that is ready to be turned over to the president and other policy makers. To create it, the IC presents the processed information to military strategists, librarians, mathematicians, and other expert analysts. They work quickly and carefully to determine what each piece of information means to the United States.

Mistakes can be made during this part of the process. Analysis can be affected by human errors in judgment. For example, two experts may disagree on what a terrorist leader's next move will be. They use the information they are given to make the best guesses that they can. But

National Intelligence Estimates

One way that intelligence is shared is through documents known as National Intelligence Estimates. Experts throughout the IC write these reports to provide in-depth looks at hot topics such as who might be close to building a nuclear bomb or which terrorist groups are likely to become stronger. National Intelligence Estimates are distributed to the president and other top leaders. They are not shared with the public because they usually contain secret information.

Maps are an important part of planning military operations.

because human behavior is unpredictable, it is impossible to be certain about what will happen in the future.

What Is Good Intelligence?

Some intelligence collected by the IC is never passed on to policy makers. That's because not all intelligence is good intelligence. The IC carefully decides which information should be sent to the president and other policy makers.

Good intelligence must be accurate. If the information is not accurate, it could be worse than useless. It might even prove harmful. For example, outdated maps could lead to disaster when planning a military attack in a foreign country.

Intelligence must also be complete to be useful. Intelligence on a subject should include all of the information that is available from each agency within the IC. Pieces of information that are not tied together could lead to incomplete or incorrect ideas about an important issue.

Good intelligence is always timely. Intelligence that is received too late to be acted upon is useless. For example, a September 10, 2001, telephone message from a suspected terrorist warned that the following day would be "zero hour." Unfortunately, the message was in a foreign language and was not translated until after the 9/11 attacks.

Intelligence should always be unbiased. This means that it should not be influenced by the opinions of anyone involved in the process. Intelligence experts should analyze the information they receive in a neutral way.

Finally, the very best intelligence is specific. Specific information might include exact details of where, when, and how a terrorist group plans to attack. This kind of information is very difficult to come by.

The Final Step: Delivering Intelligence

The fifth and final step in the intelligence process is delivering the finished intelligence. After the analysts

YESTERDAY'S HEADLINES

On August 6, 2001, President George W. Bush received a President's Daily Brief entitled "Bin Laden Determined to Strike in US." The memo showed that intelligence agencies believed that al-Qaeda might use planes to attack targets on U.S. soil. After the memo's existence was discovered, Secretary of State Condoleezza Rice and President Bush were questioned on why they hadn't reacted more swiftly to the memo. Both answered that it was well known that bin Laden wanted to attack targets in the United States, but that the PDB did not contain information about any specific threat.

have assessed the information, it must be put into a form that will be easily understood by those reading it. Intelligence is delivered to top officials in many different formats, including written memos, in-depth reports, or short verbal summaries.

One way intelligence is delivered is through the President's Daily Brief, or PDB. The PDB is a top secret report that is given each day to the president and certain other officials. Some of the information may need to be acted upon immediately. Other parts of the PDB provide answers to the questions that the president and the National Security Council (NSC) asked at the beginning of the intelligence cycle.

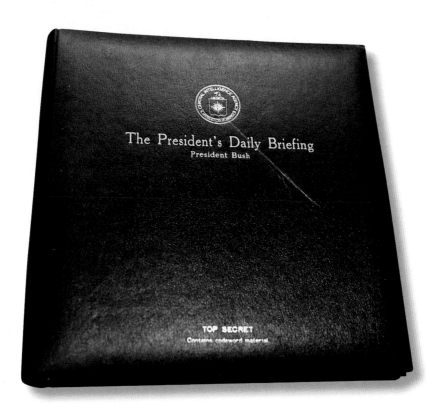

The President's Daily Brief is one of the main ways intelligence is delivered to the president.

The intelligence cycle is a never-ending process. It begins all over again as the president and the NSC request information on new issues or additional information on findings detailed in the reports.

A FIRSTHAND LOOK AT
THE PRESIDENT'S DAILY BRIEF

On April 10, 2004, President Bush released a portion of his PDB from August 6, 2001, to the public. He was the first president ever to do this while in office. The released PDB details the warning from the CIA that Osama bin Laden was planning an attack on the United States. See page 60 for a link to read the PDB online.

CHAPTER 5

HOT TOPICS

In recent years, IC leaders such as Janet Napolitano, shown here, have testified before Congress on the issue of intelligence reform.

THE PUBLIC USUALLY ONLY

hears about intelligence activities when there is an intelligence failure or a problem within the IC. The community's many successes often go unreported.

The very nature of intelligence collection covers the IC in secrecy and mystery. A government report written in 2004 described the IC as "too complex and secret." Americans often wonder how the agencies actually operate and what takes place in this hidden side of the U.S. government. In recent years, the IC has been at the center of a number of troubling controversies.

Congressional hearings in the 1970s led to major changes in how the IC is allowed to operate.

Violations of Civil Rights

Intelligence agencies must find a balance between protecting Americans' freedom from fear and making sure that their **civil rights** are not violated. By law, intelligence agencies are not allowed to deliberately collect private information on U.S. citizens or other people in the United States without **warrants**.

Before the mid-1970s, few Americans worried that intelligence agencies were violating their civil rights. But in 1975, people learned that the CIA, FBI, and other intelligence agencies had been illegally spying on some U.S. citizens. For example, many Americans who protested the Vietnam War or took part in the civil rights movement were illegally targeted for investigation.

This illegal spying made Americans suspicious of intelligence agencies. In response, Congress created several permanent committees to oversee the IC. The Senate and the House of Representatives each have a committee whose chief goal is to monitor and regulate intelligence activities.

Intelligence agencies still sometimes break the rules. In 2005, it was revealed that the National Security Agency (NSA) had been conducting a "domestic eavesdropping" program since early 2002. Called the Terrorist **Surveillance** Program, its stated goal was to find al-Qaeda connections in the United States. The NSA intercepted and screened all phone calls and e-mails between people in the United States and people in foreign countries. This was done with the president's permission but without warrants. The program was ended in 2007.

A FIRSTHAND LOOK AT
THE PRIVACY ACT OF 1974

The Privacy Act of 1974 created strict rules for how government agencies are allowed to collect, store, and use information about U.S. citizens. See page 60 for a link to read the full text of the act online.

Interrogation Techniques vs. Torture

In recent years, some agencies have been caught using controversial methods to collect intelligence. To obtain information that might save human lives, some agents have used harsh **interrogation** methods that cause physical or mental pain. While some argue that these methods are necessary, others believe they are a form of **torture**.

One controversial method used in interrogation is waterboarding. Waterboarding consists of strapping a prisoner to a tilted board, wrapping plastic or cloth around his face, and then pouring water over his head. This makes the prisoner feel like he is drowning. Waterboarding was

The harsh treatment of prisoners at the U.S. military prison at Guantanamo Bay, Cuba, has been a major source of controversy.

first authorized in early 2002. It has been used on suspected terrorists to try to gain information. Other suspected terrorists have been slapped, deprived of sleep, and forced to listen to extremely loud music for long periods of time.

Another controversial practice is known as extraordinary rendition. This process begins when U.S. agents kidnap a suspect off the streets of a foreign country. The suspect is then transported to a second foreign nation to be interrogated. Authorities in the second country are free to use whatever means they have within their power to question the prisoner. These countries have less strict laws about interrogation methods than the United States does. This means that

A VIEW FROM ABROAD

The Council of Europe Parliamentary Assembly investigated extraordinary rendition in 2006. The council's report proclaimed that "by depriving hundreds of suspects of their basic rights, including the right to a fair trial, the United States has done a disservice to the cause of justice." It also expressed the council's wish that the United States would set a better example for other nations by using more peaceful methods of gathering intelligence.

Recent studies have shown that harsh interrogation is less effective than other collection methods. Many experts believe that suspects will confess to anything under torture. In addition, methods such as waterboarding and extraordinary rendition violate the democratic principles that the United States was founded upon.

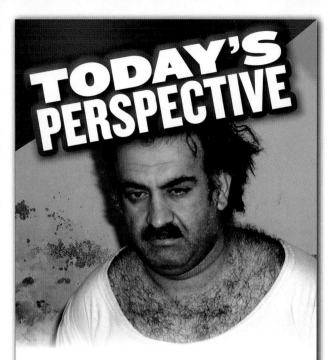

TODAY'S PERSPECTIVE

Some people believe that the government should use harsh interrogation methods if they effectively gain information that could protect our nation. But many others disagree with this viewpoint. On May 4, 2011, the *New York Times* published an editorial speaking out against violent interrogation methods. The editorial points out that tortured captives are not a reliable source of information. For example, al-Qaeda member Khalid Sheikh Mohammed (above) gave false information to U.S. agents after being waterboarded 183 times. The *Times* editorial goes on to suggest that "most experienced interrogators think that the same information, or better, can be obtained through legal and humane means."

captured suspects are often tortured.

In February 2003, U.S. agents snatched a man named Hassan Mustafa Osama Nasr from a street in Italy. Nasr was flown to Egypt, where he says he was tortured and imprisoned. In 2009, an Italian court found 22 American intelligence agents and an air force colonel guilty of Nasr's abduction. They were sentenced to between five and eight years in Italian prisons. But the Americans never showed up for the trial and still haven't turned themselves in to serve their time.

Responding to Criticism

So who is ultimately responsible for making

sure that intelligence agencies work within the laws of the United States? The president and Congress have some oversight of the IC. But the IC is also responsible for policing itself.

The ODNI has a special branch called the Office of Privacy and Civil Liberties. This office works to ensure that the IC follows all rules and government regulations concerning civil liberties. Its goal is to establish trust with the American people.

The balance between obtaining secret information and protecting civil rights is a delicate one. Policy makers and intelligence experts continue to look for answers that will satisfy all the concerns.

Hassan Mustafa Osama Nasr says he was tortured in Egypt after U.S. officials captured him on suspicion of being a terrorist.

MAP OF THE EVENTS

What Happened Where?

CANADA

UNITED
STATES

MEXICO

*ATLANTIC
OCEAN*

Mexico In recent years, powerful drug
gangs have caused an increase in deaths
and violence in Mexico. Intelligence experts
try to prevent this violence from spilling over
the border into the United States.

BRAZIL

In today's world, the disputes and disagreements of nations thousands of miles
away can still affect life in the United States. In today's global society, everyone is
connected through trade, culture, and communications. This map shows global hot
spots that might be receiving attention from the U.S. intelligence community.

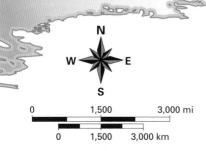

N
W E
S

| 0 | 1,500 | 3,000 mi |

| 0 | 1,500 | 3,000 km |

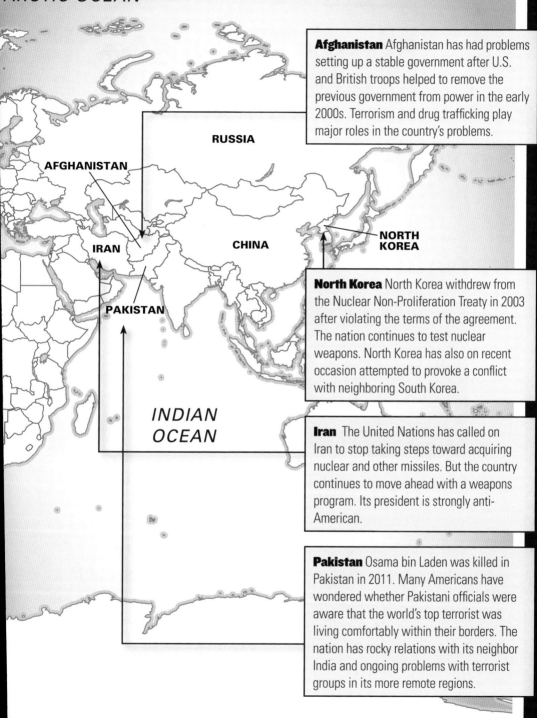

ARCTIC OCEAN

RUSSIA

AFGHANISTAN

IRAN

CHINA

NORTH KOREA

PAKISTAN

INDIAN OCEAN

Afghanistan Afghanistan has had problems setting up a stable government after U.S. and British troops helped to remove the previous government from power in the early 2000s. Terrorism and drug trafficking play major roles in the country's problems.

North Korea North Korea withdrew from the Nuclear Non-Proliferation Treaty in 2003 after violating the terms of the agreement. The nation continues to test nuclear weapons. North Korea has also on recent occasion attempted to provoke a conflict with neighboring South Korea.

Iran The United Nations has called on Iran to stop taking steps toward acquiring nuclear and other missiles. But the country continues to move ahead with a weapons program. Its president is strongly anti-American.

Pakistan Osama bin Laden was killed in Pakistan in 2011. Many Americans have wondered whether Pakistani officials were aware that the world's top terrorist was living comfortably within their borders. The nation has rocky relations with its neighbor India and ongoing problems with terrorist groups in its more remote regions.

New Threats

Some Americans celebrated the death of Osama bin Laden.

The raid on Osama bin Laden's compound in Pakistan was a huge success for the IC. The attack increased America's confidence in its intelligence agencies. It also brought a sense of closure to one of the worst chapters in U.S. history—the terrorist attacks of September 11, 2001.

In addition to ending bin Laden's violent career, the raid also resulted in the recovery of documents and computers. These items are still in the process of being examined and analyzed. Information from the confiscated goods will lead to a deeper understanding of al-Qaeda and other terrorist groups. It may also help the United States put an end to al-Qaeda.

After September 11, 2001, Americans were fearful that another terrorist attack could cause death and destruction on U.S. soil. Some experts believe that the United States is safer from large-scale violent attacks than ever before. But many people feel helpless against ever-evolving threats of terrorism, cyberattacks, and other disasters.

As long as there are people, groups, and nations that threaten the United States, the U.S. intelligence community will continue its work.

Today, a memorial stands at the former site of the World Trade Center towers, which were destroyed in the 9/11 attacks.

FOR THE DESIGN OF THE 9/11 MEMORIAL.

INFLUENTIAL INDIVIDUALS

Oleg Penkovsky

Oleg Penkovsky (1919–1963) was a Soviet military officer who spied for the United States in the early 1960s. The Soviet government tried and executed him after discovering his treason.

James Clapper (1941–) is the fourth director of national intelligence. He was appointed by President Barack Obama in August 2010.

George W. Bush (1946–) was the 43rd president of the United States. He served from 2001 to 2009. He was president during the 9/11 terrorist attacks and the beginning of the Iraq War.

Condoleezza Rice (1954–) served as secretary of state under President George W. Bush from 2005 to 2009. She was the first African American woman to hold the position. She presently teaches at Stanford University.

Osama bin Laden (1957–2011) founded the terrorist group al-Qaeda and was the mastermind behind the September 11 terrorist attacks in the United States. He was killed by the U.S. military in May 2011.

Barack Obama (1961–) is the 44th president of the United States. He has pushed the intelligence community to be more open and transparent.

Hassan Mustafa Osama Nasr (1963–) is a suspected terrorist who was illegally abducted from Italy by U.S. agents and taken to Egypt, where he was reportedly tortured.

Osama bin Laden

Barack Obama

TIMELINE

1942

The Office of Strategic Services (OSS) becomes the first centralized intelligence agency in the United States.

Mid-1940s

The Cold War between the United States and the Soviet Union begins.

2001

On September 11, al-Qaeda terrorists attack the World Trade Center in New York and the Pentagon near Washington, D.C., and are the cause of a downed plane in Pennsylvania.

2002

Iraqi spy Rafid Ahmed Alwan al-Janabi gives false information about the presence of WMDs in Iraq. The information is used to justify a war with Iraq.

2004

The Office of the Director of National Intelligence is created in response to 9/11.

1961

Soviet officer Oleg Penkovsky feeds important information to the United States about nuclear missiles in Cuba.

1963

Penkovsky is executed by the Soviets for treason.

1991

The Cold War ends with the breakup of the Soviet Union.

2010

In August, intelligence agencies trace one of Osama bin Laden's associates to a secluded house in Abbottabad, Pakistan.

2011

On May 1, Navy SEALs attack and kill Osama bin Laden at his hideout in Abbottabad.

LIVING HISTORY

Primary sources provide firsthand evidence about a topic. Witnesses to a historical event create primary sources. They include autobiographies, newspaper reports of the time, oral histories, photographs, and memoirs. A secondary source analyzes primary sources, and is one step or more removed from the event. Secondary sources include textbooks, encyclopedias, and commentaries. Visit www.factsfornow.scholastic.com for links to view these sources online. Enter the keywords **National Intelligence** and look for the Living History logo Σ̈.

Σ̈ The CIA's Penkovsky Memo Soviet military officer Oleg Penkovsky provided important intelligence to the United States in the early 1960s. When this was discovered by the Soviet government, U.S. officials expressed concern for Penkovsky's safety. You can read an official CIA memo about the incident online.

Σ̈ The Intelligence Reform and Terrorism Prevention Act of 2004 The Intelligence Reform and Terrorism Prevention Act of 2004 changed the way the IC was organized by creating the ODNI.

Σ̈ The Nuclear Non-Proliferation Treaty The Nuclear Non-Proliferation Treaty was first signed in 1968. Since then, a total of 189 nations have agreed to stop creating nuclear weapons.

Σ̈ The President's Daily Brief The President's Daily Briefs are rarely shared with the public. But in 2004, President George W. Bush shared an important piece of a 2001 brief about Osama bin Laden's potential plans for a terrorist attack on the United States.

Σ̈ The Privacy Act of 1974 The Privacy Act of 1974 established clear rules for how government agencies were allowed to gather and use information about U.S. citizens.

RESOURCES

Books

Deary, Terry. *Spies*. London: Scholastic, 2011.

Earnest, Peter. *The Real Spy's Guide to Becoming a Spy*. New York: Abrams Books for Young Readers, 2009.

Lockwood, Brad. *Domestic Spying and Wiretapping*. New York: Rosen Publishing, 2007.

Streissguth, Thomas. *America's Security Agencies: The Department of Homeland Security, FBI, NSA, and CIA*. Berkeley Heights, NJ: MyReportLinks.com Books, 2008.

Wagner, Heather Lehr. *The Federal Bureau of Investigation*. New York: Chelsea House, 2007.

**Visit this Scholastic Web site for more information on National Intelligence:
www.factsfornow.scholastic.com
Enter keywords National Intelligence**

GLOSSARY

civil rights (SIV-uhl RITES) rights that are guaranteed to all Americans by the U.S. Constitution, including freedom of speech and religion

classified (KLAS-uh-fide) declared secret by the government or other authority

counterintelligence (koun-tur-in-TEL-uh-junce) the prevention of foreign or enemy groups from stealing information

drones (DROHNZ) military aircraft without pilots that are often used for surveillance

foreign nationals (FOR-uhn NASH-uh-nuhlz) citizens of foreign countries

hackers (HAK-urz) people who are skilled at getting into computer systems without permission

infiltrate (IN-fil-trayt) sneak into

infrastructure (IN-fruh-struk-chur) the underlying systems that allow something to function

interrogation (in-ter-uh-GAY-shuhn) detailed questioning

sabotage (SAB-uh-tahzh) deliberate damage or destruction of property, especially to prevent or stop something

surveillance (sur-VAY-luhns) close observation

terrorist (TARE-ur-ist) a person who uses violence to frighten people, obtain power, or force a government to do something

torture (TOR-chur) deliberately causing extreme pain or mental suffering as punishment or to force someone to do or say something

treason (TREE-zuhn) the crime of betraying one's own country

warrants (WOR-uhnts) official documents that give permission for something, such as searching or arresting someone

INDEX

Page numbers in *italics* indicate illustrations.

ABOUT THE AUTHOR

Robin S. Doak has a bachelor's degree in English from the University of Connecticut. She has been writing for children for more than 20 years.